Comfort My Soul

Comfort My Soul

by

Janice Creasy Bradley

DORRANCE PUBLISHING CO., INC.
PITTSBURGH, PENNSYLVANIA 15222

ISBN # 0-8059-5264-0
Printed in the United States of America

First Printing

For information or to order additional books, please write:
Dorrance Publishing Co., Inc.
643 Smithfield Street
Pittsburgh, Pennsylvania 15222
U.S.A.
1 800 788 7654
Or visit our web site and on-line catalog at *www.dorrancepublishing.com*

To the heroic firefighters, victims and their families
of the September 11, 2001 tragedy.
To the United States of America and all Nations.

To Benjamin, mighty in wisdom; Shawn, a peacemaker;
Quincy, a cheerful giver.
To my virtuous mother, Viola Randolph Creasy.
To my dear brother and mentor, Lieutenant Colonel
Joseph Louis Creasy.

Contents

Acknowledgments

Glory and praise to my
Lord and Savior Jesus Christ.

The most precious person that lives, the Holy Spirit:
I give my love to thee today, yesterday and tomorrow.

Introduction

With intellectual abilities and discernment of knowledge and wisdom from God, each word created and established in this book is presented to me from the divine guidance of the Holy Spirit.

May the reading of this book *Comfort Your Soul.*

Comfort My Soul

Father wrap your heavenly arms around me.
Drink my tears that they may be emptied by
The touch of your powerful hands.
Hold me; caress me.
Gently pick me up from whence forth I come.
For my body is weak; my heart is weary
Comfort my soul.

A Rose for You for Being a Rose for Me

Holding this rose in my hand as my tear
drops from my cheeks covers its
blossoms giving it strength to grow.
Your unique spirit embodies my forbidden soul
while I await patiently for
the love of this rose.
My heart feels the presence of your divine
love that echoes from the
almighty above.
This rose I will cherish with grace shall
always be a part of me: this rose
from you to me shall carry us to our destiny.
For this rose: this precious rose:
a rose for you for being a rose for me.

A Good Soldier

A good soldier is one who allows grace to stand against all
evil forces and the darkness of this world.

He upholds his integrity with armor and shields of
protection, diligently seeking
peace, love, and prosperity among all nations.

He wears the helmet of wisdom and honor to protect
him from the unjust and to
discern the heart of the iniquity.

He is whipped spontaneously, the spirit of his body
bruised by many false illusions
but yet he maintains his strength with faith and courage
to climb the highest mountain of salvation.

He walks in the heat of sunlight with sweat dripping
from his brow as his soul
thirsts for the breastplate of righteousness.

His footsteps and admiration of his weapons are
embodied with dignity and boldness
of the many battle grounds of victory.

He stands gracefully with his sword in his right hand
looking upward to the sky
with visions of defeat in his eyes that God shall redeem
the weakness of man and exalt the courage of men.

The Vine of God

Open your eyes and what do you see?
All that God has restored unto me.

From the earth I came and the presence within,
It was known that life was to begin.

My eyes are open now I see;
The truth is the way it will always be.

He waters my soul and makes me strong;
Bringing me up to know right from wrong.

When I fall He will pick me up;
And bless my spirit with an anointing cup.

Like a leaf I will wither and hang below;
He'll give me strength and I will continue to grow.

Peace and Joy shall sustain my fruit;
Thy seed is my seed; my root thy root.

Now you let my light so shine;
I must hold on to this vine;

Lord, please keep my leaf green.

Grace

She looked upon the countenance
of my soul;

Her heart felt the emptiness
of my sacred love;

The smile upon her face was gentle and kind
with all the beautiful colors surrounding
her vibrant and canny spirit.

The wisdom she possessed embraced the essence
of my cry.

Her spirit captured my heart as I watched her
vanish away.

A Man's Cry

They cry out for love when it's not there trying
to withhold the substance of their mortal being within.
Yearning for love deep within their soul.

His strength becomes weak, yet strong enough to prevail
the calamities.

He is exalted from his youth to conquer the battlegrounds of love.

His wisdom is worn with justice and faith seeking
manifestation of his beloved.

His voice is like thunder miraculously escaping the depths of pain as
he yearns to find the rib of his flesh.

He walks through the quiet darkness of night trying to discern the
loneliness of his heart; desiring to be nurtured by the beauty he sees.

The memories of his tears are cast into the waters of yesterday and
renewed in the fountain of grace.
His gentle heart wanting to be loved by the flowers of birth.

Stand firm graciously as a man; don't let the sun close your eyelids.

Lift your head up, you strong man, and let the softness of her eyes
caress the emptiness in your heart.

Friendship with God

Let the Lord thy God remain within
Abide in his love
From heaven above.

Be faithful with patience and wait
For His call
He is the one who loves us all.

When He speaks to us we deny Him and go our separate ways;
Wandering afar in distance each day.

When our body becomes weak with little hope and less to hold;
Joy and peace shall comfort our souls.

All His love and wisdom shows that He cares;
For he will strengthen us in things we cannot bare.

Then will I say my God where have you been;
My child I have not gone away;
I am here always to stay with you forever,
Day by day.

Holy Spirit

I don't know you, yet I do.
I've never met you, although I feel you.
I can't find you, but you are beside me.
Your spirit touches me, but I can't see you.
Your heart cries for me, but I can't hold you.
You hear me speak, but I see no audience.
You guide my walk; your footprints I cannot find.

Candlelight

As the candle burns upon its flame,
So does the tears of my heart cry out to thee;
That I may see the light of this candle, Jesus;
Who dwells so deep within my soul.

The Greatest is Love

From my heart, Oh God, from my heart, I love thee now, I love thee
yesterday, and tomorrow. Your love is with everlasting power.
No love is greater than this love because it comes
from heaven above.

Your love casts out all hate and fear with grace and
compassion that's divinely pure.

Your love speaks to us inwardly, with words of expression that
no one can define; it keeps our intellect with a spiritual mind.

Your love is not puffed up, nor is it filled with envious condemnation
or strife; but yet filled with joy, peace, and wisdom that leads to a
fruitful, content life.

Your love looked beyond our fault and saw our need, like the crying
of a newborn wanting to be freed.

Your love carried us through our trials and tribulations, restoring our
soul each night while the stars were shining from above so bright.

Your love is like the flowers that bloom each season, with their
colors and shapes so pure,
Just awaiting the overflowing power of grace to embrace their pre-
cious beauty each year.

Your love is stronger and more powerful than the wings of the eagles
that protects its nest; for this love will carry us North, South,
East, and West.

This love flows from the heart that protects us and keeps us;
for what can be greater than love itself?

Your Presence

Your presence is the candle that glows
to enlighten my heart.

Your presence is the stars that twinkle
My every breath.

Your presence is the water, I drink
to purify my body.

Your presence is the substance of nourishment unto my
belly.

Your presence is the guidance
To my daily awakening.

Your presence is my being
That you now control.

Your presence means more than
Silver and Gold.

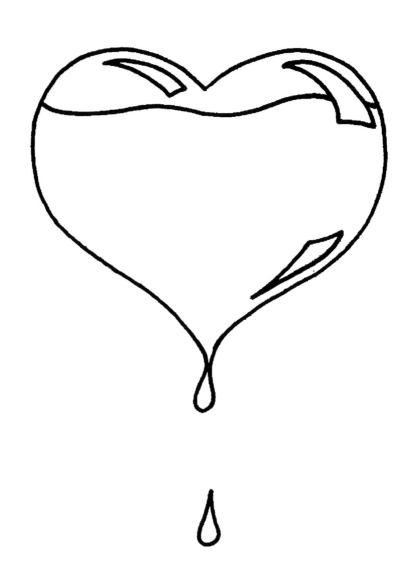

Love

Love to be love,
if they are the same,
how can it separate
itself; unless hate creeps
in and takes thee away?

Carry Me to the Cross

Father, what must I do that my soul grieves for you so.
The spirit of your presence escalates through the perfection of my
blood.
Your light gleams through the doors of my heart.
I feel as though I am dying and death is at my bed.
Lord, pick me up and take my body to the glory that lies ahead.
Strengthen me, uphold me, lead me to the promise land.
Mold me, divert me, sanctify me with the touch of thy merciful hand.
For my eyes are dim, my body is vain, carry me to the cross of Jesus.

Apple of My Heart

My heart is like the redness
of an apple.

Its beauty glows from the
seed of its core.

It is nurtured from the substance of the invisible,
but yet seen with the essence of glory.

Its sweetness is attached to the vine of integrity.

Its shape is surrounded by the characteristics of
genuine love.

It cries out to be picked up and embraced
by the hands of mercy.

It is tossed about seeking to indwell in the
presence of hope.

Yet its scars and bruises glows like the
redness of my heart.

The Chosen Path

Because I speak not after the things of the world;
But of the goodness of the things in heaven.

Then shall I attain my spirit
To the Holy Ghost and
Abstain my spirit from the adversary.

For I will not be afflicted by the evil spirits;
They soon will be cast
Into the land of dry bones.

And I will lift mine eyes upon thee;
And open my heart and mind
With the love of God flowing
Into my conscious and my soul.

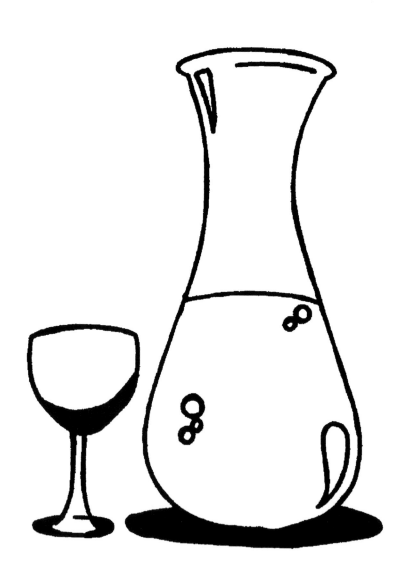

Inspirations of Love

He delivered me from my mother's womb.
Gave me drink from the spirit of life;
Filled my heart with inspirations of love.
Consumed my tears in the palm of his hands;
Opened my eyes to see the truth of wisdom.
Fed my soul from the platter of grace;
Watches over me from the beginning of birth.

Son of Man

Peace be still, for the word of-the Lord has come upon me that I am son of man.

My heart grieves with much love for thee. The blood that flows within my body fills my anointed vessels with dignity and prosperity enabling me to look up to the most high with justice and redemption.

My light is like the candle that burns so bright that passeth through the heart of man, some have fallen, some will remain fallen. For my God who acknowledges the pure heart shall lift thee up and carry thee with him to the light of salvation.

For the spirit of-the Lord is upon me. My soul, my heart, my mind, I beseech thee to guide me through the pathway of destruction and exalt my body and all who may follow to the throne of grace and mercy.

For a fool no not God, but a righteous man, his ear will be eager to hear the word and the word is my Lord Jesus Christ. For at the point of this world was the word and so shall it be at the end. For the righteous man bows his head with loyalty and sings from his heart with grace.

Meek

The words you speak are precious and pure;
They bring the truth to the listening ear.
The breath you breathe from God above,
enables you to exalt in his love.
The light you let shine is filled with grace
with memories of tomorrow and dreams
to embrace.

I'm Going Back to Jesus

I'm going back to Jerusalem as far as I can see;
I'm going back to see Jesus to claim my victory.

I struggled many days and nights to see his mighty face;
The spirit that kept me in his care was the amazing grace.

I tossed and turned in the lonely nights to find my face in tears;
But when I looked up to heaven, I knew I had nothing to fear.

It was his precious love that carried me along the way;
He gave his life that I may live, my heart is with him today.

I could not bear these burdens alone with all the pain and strife;
Jesus has come to save my soul and to give me a brand new life.

Because I kept my faith in him and in him did I trust;
My life is guided by the spirit of love who seeks to dwell in us.

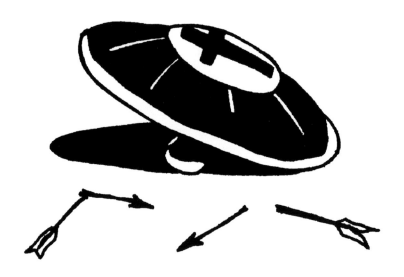

Oh Divine

Your smile enlightens the world around you
giving it the presence of glory.

Your strength is powerful with shields of
protection captivating each heartbeat that falls.

The enchantment of your spirit sends messages
to the fulfillment of my flesh.

Your walk is justified by integrity and grace.

The wisdom of your eyes seeks
to dominate the essence of my heart.

The loyalty you possess is guided
by the angels of light.

Your gentle touch embraces the depths
of my forbidden soul.

Green Leaves

Green leaves you are,
hanging there all alone;
yet not alone,
but desolate.
Your presence stares,
speaks to me silently
with words of emotions.

Sacred Grounds

As I sat on the grounds of mercy and holiness,
the sun revealing its shadow; my soul desiring to
be comforted by the presence of his sheep;
the trees discerning the countenance of my spirit,
I await patiently for the ladies of worship to welcome
me to their anointed kingdom. The stillness of the air
is filled with sweetness as I breathe in the sounds of glory.
The birds sing halleluia, flapping their wings to the
winds of grace.

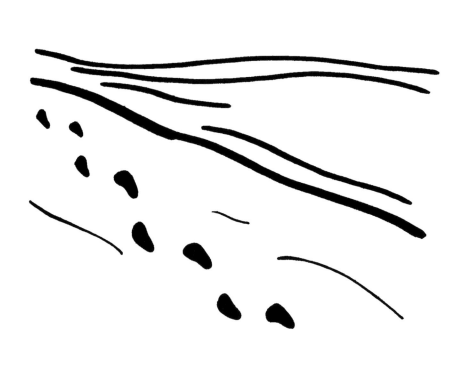

I Will

I will sing songs of praise unto his holy name and he shall
enlighten my soul with joy from above.

I will gather up thorns and thistles of enmity and transgressions
and carry them to the temple of divine worship.

I will cast all my burdens of grief and sorrow
upon the resting place of his bosom.

I will follow him through the valley of dry waters
to the omnipotent flooded lands of peace and justice.

I will walk in the pathway of the body of Christ
and escape the footprints of the iniquity of man.

Then will I magnify my voice with the angels in heaven
around me and above me; and the sound of the
trumpet will be echoed into the earth.

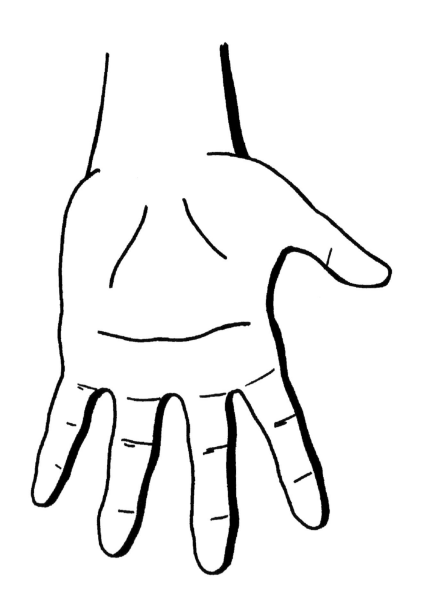

The Five Senses

To *hear* the birds sing from their hearts
with harmony of joy.

To *see* the sky with movements of ecstasy
as the clouds form each rain drop that falls.

To *feel* the presence of the wind that penetrates
the depths of one's soul.

To *smell* the beauty and elegance of the flowers
that bloom from the stillness of their buds.

To *taste* the sweetness of the honeysuckle as
they await eagerly to be born.

A Man's Spirit

I knew a man's spirit deep in my soul;
His voice lifted my burdens and carried me as the days grew old.

His light was let shown from the angels above,
that gave him harmony with music of love.

His most gracious spirit and gentle voice
was anointed with thanksgiving to praise and rejoice.

He was exulted above many men high and low;
to sing to the world; Jesus is with me wherever I go!

I saw this man in a vision of light;
His reflection of strength as a candle that burns through the night.

As I bowed my head to receive God's grace;
The spirit of his eyes was upon my face.

Then I looked up and saw no more;
But there he was standing at the door.

Lord, Here I Am

The shadow you left behind caught up with me and carried me
to the place of my destiny.

It sat me on a pillar of rock, my eyes staring
towards the gates of Heaven.

My body feeble, desiring the true comfort of love.

Trying to elude from the agility of its presence; I could not escape.

Suddenly I lifted up my hands and cried.
Lord, here I am.

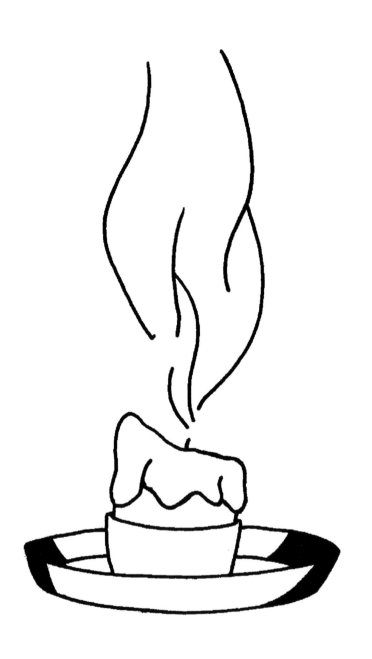

Give Me Drink From the Cup of Life

When I awake in the mornings and adjust myself to my daily guide,
My spirit is up and around; I look back and my body is still there
Wavering in pain and grief.

My spirit has come out of my body; it stares at me
Wondering, watching, what shall I do
It says I have been tossing to and fro upon the earth.

The flesh of my bones lay still like the sand in the ocean,
Awaiting God to reform my eternal being
That it may be lifted up and made whole again.

My eyes are filled with darkness of day,
Like the candle that has no light

My dreams are like sour grapes; they are not sweet,
My morning awakening
Is filled with desolation from my enduring and feeble heart.

My hairs upon my head are as snowflakes covering my shoulders
And changing
With the seasons that's granted from above.

My teeth are white and pure; yet clinched together
Too weak to absorb the breath of life.

My hands are gentle and soft like the clouds in the sky;
only able to lift one fingertip to each rain drop that falls.

My breasts are full and ripened with sweet milk and honey
Just awaiting to be nurtured by the touch of his holy hands.

My spirit is restless, my soul thirsts after thee,
Give me drink from the cup of life.

A Child's Heart!

I looked at my child, I say,
"Why are you listening to that style of music?"
His innocent eyes look at me and stares;
Yet his soul confused not knowing where to find life.
His walk is bold and upright with trousers swaying with the
winds of the world, not being able to distinguish the identify
of his true being. I say, Lord, forgive him for he does not
know yet between the times of these two lives.
But you and only you know his precious heart belongs to you."

My First Love

You are my first love;
The love that shall always be
The love that dwells
Inside my soul;
Is the love
That was given to me.

Gentle Thistles

As I gathered my hand and pulled the cotton from the thistles
with sweat dripping from my brow;

The sun shining on my back as the reflection of the heat refuse
to cast its shadow from the numbness of my body,

The whiteness of the cotton staring me in the face as though it could
speak to me; it says, "Let not your heart be sad with me,
for I am your friend."

Then it says to me once again; "Please be my friend,
for you are the beginning and so shall you be the end."

Yet, I Was Persecuted

I assist them, yes I comforted them,
my hands labored upon the iniquities of their deceitful hearts.
I gently caressed the wickedness of their tongues.
My spirit vexed by the animosity of their bones.
Bitterness beguiled their forbidden soul as they sought to
destroy the most inner part of my being.
The calamities of their heart seeked to distress me while
I filled their cup with love.
Yet, I was persecuted.

Release Me, Oh Father

I see this thing in my life, it bites me all the day long.
My body is covered with wepts and grief.
I say to it go away, please go away.
Desperately wanting it to disappear,
it continues to cling to my mortal body.
my spirit desiring to be strong, I reach out for life and cry out to
My heavenly father to release me from this conspicuous enemy.

Birth of a Snowflake

As the snowflakes fall from heaven the trees eagerly await the
identify of their gentle touch.

The flakes appear to be cold and dreadful but to the trees they are
comfort to their lonely and desolate hearts.

The swiftness of their presence accumulates
the grounds of mercy.

The stillness of the wind shuts its doors giving each flake authority
to preserve every heartbeat of its kind.

The sun refuses to shine so that eyes may see the beauty of
its creation.

The clouds hide their faces behind the sun as they peek with
anticipation to renew their birth.

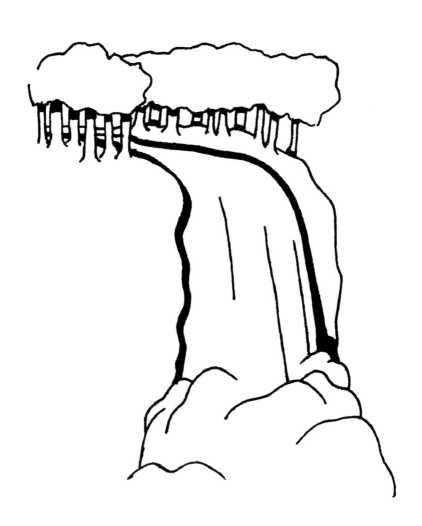

Sobriety

You came to me as a child with a dream;
The sound of your voice escalating like the water,
from a sounding stream.

Attracted by the spirit of your conscious;
Your characteristics so gentle and meticulous.

Miraculously seeking destination
of perfection and grace;
With contentment in your heart and sobriety upon your face.

Abiding in hope for promises from above;
Anxiously awaiting the gift of love.

Let Me Live

Let me live, oh Lord
I shalt not die;
I gave you my best cry.

Let me live, oh Lord
I struggled for a fresh drink of heaven's water.
My heart yearns to see the joy of laughter.

Let me live, oh Lord,
I labored in the fields of sunlight.
I hugged my tears through each lonely and feeble night.

Let me live, oh Lord,
I walked through the storms of grief and injustice.
I escaped the road of endless.

Let me live, oh Lord.
I carried the prints of my footsteps.
I slept at the rich folks doorsteps.

Let me live, oh Lord,
I endured the iniquities of strength.
My faith goes beyond the measurements of its length.

Let me live, oh Lord,
I loved my neighbor's enemy.

Let me live,
live my destiny.

Oh Lord,
Let me live.

Insights for the Heart and Soul

I will not fall from the grace of God, nor will I allow my light to be turned into darkness.

❋ ❋ ❋

I count not myself as who I am, but who I may become.

❋ ❋ ❋

I seek not to gain for myself, but to contribute my gifts to Christ Jesus.

❋ ❋ ❋

Once I know the ways of God, then will I know who I am.

❋ ❋ ❋

Beware of the bad thoughts so that the goodness of the mind may be established.

❋ ❋ ❋

With all earnest expectations that I may sovereign dwell in God's grace.

❋ ❋ ❋

My life in this world is filled with the many wonders and mysteries of the illumination of my hopes and dreams.

*** *** ***

The holy spirit is here on earth with us now. He abides in
our hearts when we let him in.

*** *** ***

Beauty is of God and the presence within; God is a God of beauty.

*** *** ***

The grace of God shall withstand all the iniquities and vanities of life.

*** *** ***

God's best friend is the heart that shows love.

*** *** ***

I fear God for the good that I do not do; but the good that I
do, I do not fear him.

*** *** ***

Love is the fulfillment of the heart to all that believeth.

*** *** ***

Show me your way, oh God, that I may walk in your footsteps.

*** *** ***

Blessed are those who sing melody of the Holy Spirit.

*** *** ***

Even though I am far away, my heart is beside yours in grace.

* * *

Wavering faith is like a ship coasting upon the waves of the ocean;
Whereas solid faith is like the swiftness of an arrow into the sky.

* * *

The heart is the spirit of God, a manifestation of his love.

* * *

God lives in our hearts which is the source and power that keeps us
alive.

* * *

The beginning of life is the heart and so is the end.

* * *

Open your heart to the invisible love.

* * *

I am a warrior for Christ.

* * *

Be silent sometimes and listen to what God has to say;
we often wonder why God does not respond to our daily
needs; it is because we do not open our listening ears
to his spiritual voice.

* * *

Similarities to keep in our hearts;
Peace, Serenity, Hope
Love, Justice, Faith

* * *

Enhance my dreams, Let my memories of yesterday be
uplifted by the enchantment of your spirit.

* * *

The less pain I subdue, the weaker my faith;
The more pain I endure, the stronger my faith.

* * *

God's spirit is with me when I speak;
His spirit touches the spirit of others
when my words are uttered.

* * *

The more wisdom he gives me, the greater my works;
The less wisdom l obtain; the smaller my tasks.

* * *

By his spirit I seek not vengeance nor persecution;
but righteousness unto all men.

* * *

If thy give of oneself; then shall he also receive of another.

* * *

If you show a Christian respect;
thou shall receive respect.
If thou show a fool respect;
he will not receive it to himself;
nor will he manifest it to others.

* * *

Obedience and devotion to God allows a righteous
man to inherit the law of God.

∗ ∗ ∗

A home is moral principles characterized by love.

∗ ∗ ∗

To exceed in this world and excel in God's world.

∗ ∗ ∗

For their eyes are of misery and pain, their ears are feeble;
too content to allow grace to abide in their heart.

∗ ∗ ∗

Everything good I do is of God, everything bad is not; therefore,
with each blink of the eye I must show myself as good.

∗ ∗ ∗

To be tempted is sweetness to its taste;
but the results are turned to bitterness.

∗ ∗ ∗

Peace I live;
Peace I die,
Love I desire;
Love I need.

∗ ∗ ∗

Your life is what you make it;
you plant your seed to grow what you are.

∗ ∗ ∗